LEE'S STREET JIU JITSU TRAINING TECHNIQUES

VOL.1 "THE ESSENTIAL DEFENSE GUIDE TO USE IN A STREET FIGHT"

WOLF

AuthorHouse™
1663 Liberty Drive
Bloomington, IN 47403
www.authorhouse.com
Phone: 1 (800) 839-8640

Because of the dynamic nature of the Internet, any web addresses or links contained in this book may have changed
since publication and may no longer be valid. The views expressed in this work are solely those of the author and do not
necessarily reflect the views of the publisher, and the publisher hereby disclaims any responsibility for them.

Any people depicted in stock imagery provided by Getty Images are models,
and such images are being used for illustrative purposes only.
Certain stock imagery © Getty Images.

Cover Image Credit: authorhousepublishing artist

This book is printed on acid-free paper.

ISBN: 978-1-7283-2317-6 (sc)
ISBN: 978-1-7283-2318-3 (e)

Library of Congress Control Number: 2019913564

Print information available on the last page.

Published by AuthorHouse 10/18/2019

authorHOUSE®

In Loving Memory

I dedicate this book in memory of my Grandmother Betty Miller Lee
(March 20, 1933 to February 14, 2015)

CONTENTS

INTRODUCTION

Through the years there has been a lot of speculation about street fighting. Also, there has been a lot of studies and emphasis on which style of martial arts is best competitive against a street fighter. Unfortunately, there has been evidence of skilled martial artists getting bested or defeated by an aggressive street fighter despite their years of skills and experience. The late great Bruce Lee said it best when he mentioned that a good boxer with a wrestling background could easily defeat a typical black belt with martial arts skills. This may be true for a number of reasons to include the discipline of the martial artists and the likelihood of him or her getting into random street fights where there are no rules, an element of the unknown and the basic concept of the individual possessing those skills that Bruce lee was talking about previously. Of course, one should never underestimate anyone but one must avoid the possibility of freezing or thinking too much when danger exists. It is true that most martial artists are very disciplined and they will only fight when instructed to do so but in a street fight this creates a totally different level of thinking and landscape. For instance, most street fights are not on the mat nor at sporting competitions, they are usually outside or inside against some psycho trying to hurt you. According to Martial Arts vs. Street Fighter Myths, "Martial Arts is something you do with somebody and hard-core street fighting you do to someone. More importantly, in street fights belts and ranks do not matter, being a black belt in some martial arts does not guarantee you that you will be successful against a younger, physically strong, rough and tough violent thug in physical battle. As a martial artist one must adapt to whatever form of violence is being used and make appropriate adjustments in order to win the fight. The worst thing that can happen when faced with a physical confrontation is to do nothing while the aggressor is challenging you to a fight, this can be perceived as cowardly, even though you may simply be thinking too much before the fight occurs.

Some martial arts are not very useful in real life street confrontations, they are proven to be more useful for fitness, self-discipline, energy and health and wellness. Those styles of martial arts do provide opportunities for individuals to learn self-defense against a would-be attacker and how to escape bad situations however if the attacker continues to engage the victim and becomes more violent, panic may set in resulting in the victim forgetting all that was taught to him or her previously. Depending on the individual's strengths and natural reflexes he or she may become fatigue during the violent exchange due to anxiety and be seriously harmed. Bruce Lee is one of my favorite martial artists because he defied all of the myths about martial arts during the 60's and 70's. Bruce Lee would make simple phrases like "boards don't hit back" or "don't think feel" and they would have such compelling meaning. To understand what he was trying to say is that you can punch bags and kick boards but you need to have an opponent in front of you to exchange strikes to see if you will be able to connect on any of your strikes. The other person may simply move out of the way or slip the punch or kick and hit you back with a more dangerous strike. In the movie Enter the Dragon Bruce Lee told the young child at the beginning of the movie, "don't think feel". Bruce Lee appeared to be saying when face to face with your opponent don't think about what you are going to do to your opponent, be first, feel it hits on it's on. In many ways, Bruce Lee is largely credited for being the first real mixed martial artists in which he blended styles from various martial arts and included elements of boxing, fencing, and Gung Fu to create his own style called jeet kune do (Tao-Jkd) "way of the intercepting fists". Bruce Lee would challenge any martial artists and street fighter in order to test his own style against theirs in order to prove superiority and the need for more full contact based martial arts.

Another example of martial arts geared towards street fighting and mixing styles was created by the Gracie Family, developed by Helio Gracie and Almeda from Brazil and Japan. Almeda from Japan was able to train Helio Gracie and teach him the Japanese form of Jiu Jitsu in which Helio was able to develop, create, compete and build various Gracie schools in the development of his own style Brazilian Jiu Jitsu. Brazilian Jiu Jitsu is a well proven martial arts style that focusses on various areas of grappling, mixed martial arts and self-defense techniques. One of the most important elements of Brazilian Jiu Jitsu are the techniques to combat a street fighter and the ability to finish the fight quickly. There is not much striking involved in Brazilian Jiu Jitsu due to it being referred to as the "gentle art". However, there are examples of strikes being used on YouTube videos where the famous Gracie challenge would take place in which different martial artists would come to the Gracie gym and challenge one of the Gracie instructors and get their ass handed to them in a nut shell. Moreover, there are other examples of some MMA schools including boxing and Muay Thai along with Brazilian Jiu Jitsu in order to create a more well-rounded system as seen in the Ultimate Fighting Championships or UFC. To compare, Bruce Lee was a huge supporter of mixing styles from various techniques in which Brazilian Jiu Jitsu does the same today. Also, both Jeet Kune Do and Brazilian Jiu Jitsu styles focus on real life combat against aggressive attackers or even multiple attackers. In the movie Enter the Dragon Bruce Lee was already adopting some elements of Jiu Jitsu into his Jeet Kune Do style when he easily submitted the much bigger opponent with an unorthodox armbar in which his opponent was forced to tap out or risk serious injury. If Bruce Lee continued to live I 'am almost certain that he would have incorporated Jiu Jitsu into his Jeet Kune Do style, at least versions that he felt would be most adequate to his form of martial art. While there has been much debate about which martial art is the best to use against a street fighter, the real answer should be a combination of techniques, utilizing Jiu Jitsu and making proper adjustments to win the fight.

In reference to the author, I' am a 45-year-old Brazilian Jiu Jitsu Purple Belt with a background in Boxing, Muay Thai, Aikido, and Mixed Martial Arts. In addition, I' am an 18-year veteran of the Alexandria Sheriff's Office in which I' am a veteran Defensive Tactics Instructor and SERT Team Member. I continue to serve in both capacities and train in the skill of martial arts. I do not believe that you have to become a black belt to teach or become a well-rounded fighter against a street fighter. In fact, I do believe that most martial arts should be geared towards fighting against street fighters or multiple attackers to prevent someone from causing you serious harm in any situation i.e. robbery, assault at a gas station, an aggressive driver assault or surprise attacker. The truth is that most martial arts is geared towards self defense due to legal laws, obligations and enrollment of students. Also, the possibilities for injuries or legal actions of civil liabilities can become a factor. In any case, the purpose of me writing this book is to provide the reader with some insight when faced with physical confrontations and provide them with tools and skills needed to defend themselves in combat hand to hand situations. For most of my career I have worked in areas of protection and public safety that required me to deal with situations in security, in the jail, on the street and at the courthouse. Each situation is never the same, I have witnessed and dealt with violent offenders trying to assault officers while on duty or situations that required my assistance to prevent a more dangerous outcome. Not all situations require you to get into a physical exchange are use your weapon. It is not wise to go around looking for fights however if one comes your way, you should be prepared to take the person on if necessary. More importantly, it is my hope this book will provide you with the skills needed to safeguard you, your family or any person you love from a would-be attacker. Furthermore, the illustrations demonstrated in this book are simply to show you a way to protect and defend yourself but not the way, the way will be your own interpretation of the techniques and which ones are most effective to you to make it your own. I have created a style called Street Jiu Jitsu to combat real life street fighting situations that I hope will prove useful to all of you.

FACE YOUR FEARS

When situations arise people will say "Oh I was not afraid, or I wasn't nervous but the reality is that fear is natural and when things happen out of the ordinary your bodies natural reaction is to be fearful until things calm down or there is no longer a threat that exists. One can be fearful and not afraid or fearful but not nervous. The importance about fear is that one must recognize it but avoid being non-responsive when danger arise. For example, your driving your car and someone hits you from behind with their vehicle. Next, they then hop out of their car cussing at you and they begin kicking your car with their foot to try to get you to come out of your vehicle. A situation like this may cause you some anxiety at first because you have no idea of who the person is or if he or she is carrying a weapon in the vehicle. In this situation you must be smart, remain in your vehicle and call the police if you do not have a phone simply drive off and do not wait for things to escalate and call the police again. However, if the individual gets back into his or her vehicle and tries to run you off the road this will give you more justification to address their aggressive behavior from a physical standpoint. Most people will not admit when they are afraid for fear of appearing cowardly however, fear is good because it alerts your body signals that something is happening out of the ordinary or that you may be in danger. Competing or fighting causes natural fear to occur however one must always be prepared to take on such challenges. Another fear can be you getting punked in front of your girlfriend, friends or significant other. Not only is it fearful but ultimately embarrassing. This can cause you to lose confidence in yourself and make you question if you where truly afraid or where you just not in the mood to fight due to some other circumstance. Either way, people like to gossip and those types of situations become over sensationalized and blown out of proportion. If you freeze and do nothing this will become even more regrettable because most will feel that you lost your heart and will to fight and that your level of skillfulness is all fake. These types of dilemmas will cause you self-doubt and you don't want that to happen you. The best way to face your fears is to be honest with yourself and understand that fear is natural. Even though you may be fearful this does not mean you should shutdown and do nothing.

One of the best ways to face your fears is to worry less about what bad can happen to you but focus on surviving the situation and winning the fight. One of the biggest issues with skilled martial artist is that even though the person may be very skillful, he or she can still freeze up because fighting and training on the mat are really two different things. This becomes easier if the martial artist competes and is used to the constant movements presented in a street fight but if you're in a usual calm and normal training environment once someone is angry and challenges you face to face this can become a problem. Usually the hesitation comes from thinking too much and not reacting to the threat in front of you which can be perceived as being afraid, fearful or even dangerous. Sometimes you may be so use to saving other people from danger that you can forget to defend and protect yourself. Of course, you should pick and choose your battles wisely and every situation does not require you to be hands on however if you are put into a position where you must protect yourself, your family or others, and talking it out does not work then worry less about the threat and focus more on combating that threat in a meaningful aggressive manner. Fear does not make cowards out of men but fatigue does, so make sure that you are training and try not to get caught off guard but if you are, practice your skills and conquer your fears.

PHILOSOPHIES

The old philosophies of street fighting were that as long as you can box and wrestle that is all you will need to be able to win in a street fight. During this time Bruce Lee would speak against martial arts schools that focused on non -contact competing. I love the phrase "boards don't hit back". In this case Bruce Lee was correct in that one may throw a strike or kick however the opponent may move or slip the strike and return a punch that may land in a way that can change the outcome of the fight. I'm not a fan of any high-flying kicks but they look nice in sport forms and on tv. High flying kicks can be dangerous to use in a street fight because you may get knocked out on your way down to the ground, low and mid-level kicks are best to use and safer in a fight exchange. Another factor Bruce Lee focused on is speed and quickness with his feet and fists. In Gracie Jiu Jitsu, part of the understanding of fighting is that most fights usually go to the ground so one should close the distance, take the opponent down and submit him or her. The fact is that all martial arts have something to offer, there are strengths and weaknesses in all. No one system is the single most effective system to use. Brazilian Jiu Jitsu has proven to be the most used in cage fights and in the UFC. Basically, no one wants to compete or should compete in any cage type match without having some type of Brazilian Jiu Jitsu background or at least have a decent ground game. Being one dimensional is not a strength, you want to be able to adapt to any style and have some level of proficiency from a combination of styles and techniques. One of the best characteristics of Brazilian Jiu

Jitsu is that you are able to stop an opponent by submission without seriously harming the other person. If you have to use lethal force there is an option for that as well. Another philosophy is that because you are a black belt you can beat anyone. Being a blackbelt is important because it shows your level of commitment to a particular art but if you are not use to being in fights there is no guarantee that you will win. The best philosophy to have is the Bruce Lee phrase "be like water be formless". This means to adapt to any style and take the form and shape it into your own style or technique. Also, if it works use it, don't dismiss other forms of martial arts because you never know what may be useful in your tool box. Be a jack of all trades, the more the merrier. If you put limits on what you think may or may not work, you will prevent yourself from growing and you will create opportunities for your opponent to defeat you since you are not familiar with certain styles and techniques.

The world of martial arts is a very large entity in which people practice different styles. Every now and then those martial arts styles compete against each other and or translated into forms of protection for those seeking to defend themselves against would be attackers or simply acquire self-defense skills. The good thing about today's martial arts is that people want to see real close contact martial arts instead of event spectator forms and non-contact martial arts. More and more, people are realizing that being well rounded is the best system to have in order to be a decent martial artist. Also, that style, weight, skills and years of training is important as well. Sometimes surviving a dangerous encounter and being alive can be the best result especially if weapons are involved. Moreover, whatever martial arts technique is chosen, one should always keep an open mind and use it as a gateway to learn other styles in order to become a more complete martial artist. Best practice is making it a part of your lifestyle. You should breathe, eat, sleep and train martial arts. Most of all, respect the art and be well disciplined, use it to help your community and yourself.

30 DAY CALENDAR/ DIET/ NUTRITION

DAY 1:   BREAKFAST- BAKED OMELET

SNACK: VANILLA SHAKE WITH BERRIES

LUNCH: TURKEY SANDWICH/ NO CHEESE/ AVOCADO/ VEGGIES

SNACK: BROWN RICE CAKE WITH VEGGIES AND SPREAD

DINNER: CROCKPOT PORK TACO'S

SNACK: APPLE/ ALMOND BUTTER

DAY 2:   BREAKFAST- OATMEAL

SNACK: VANILLA SHAKE WITH PUMPKIN

LUNCH: LEFTOVER PORK TACO'S

SNACK: VEGGIES WITH HUMMUS

DINNER: CHICKEN PARMESAN WITH WHOLE WHEAT PASTA

DAY 3:   BREAKFAST- YOGURT WITH BERRIES

SNACK: CHOCOLATE SHAKE WITH ALMOND BUTTER

LUNCH: CHICKEN SALAD WITH WATER

SNACK: COTTAGE CHEESE AND VEGGIES

DINNER: CHICKEN NOODLE SOUP

DAY 4: BREAKFAST-GRANOLA BAR

SNACK: VANILLA SHAKE WITH BERRIES

LUNCH: TACO SALAD

SNACK: BROWN RICE CAKE WITH ALMOND BUTTER AND BANANA

DINNER: CHICKEN WITH VEGGIES

DAY 5: BREAKFAST- BREAD OMELET

SNACK: CHOCOLATE WITH COCONUT EXTRACT

LUNCH: CHICKEN SOUP

SNACK: ALMOND AND ORANGE

DINNER: CHILI

DAY 6: BREAKFAST- OATMEAL WITH BERRIES

SNACK: CHOCOLATE SHAKE

LUNCH: GRILLED CHEESE ON WHOLE WHEAT/ CORN SOUP/SALAD

SNACK: STRING CHEESE

DINNER: WHOLE WHEAT SPAGHETTI WITH TURKEY MEAT

DAY 7: BREAKFAST: CEREAL

SNACK: VANILLA SHAKE WITH BERRIES

LUNCH: SALAD WITH GRILLED CHICKEN

SNACK: CELERY WITH ALMOND BUTTER

DINNER: POT PIE CHICKEN

DAY8:   BREAKFAST: YOGURT AND BANANA

SNACK: CHOCOLATE SHAKE

LUNCH: TUNA SALAD WITH VEGGIES

SNACK: CELERY STICKS WITH PEANUT BUTTER

DINNER: ROAST BEEF SANDWICH WITH STEAMED VEGGIES

DAY 9:   BREAKFAST: BOILED EGG AND APPLE

SNACK: GRANOLA BAR WITH FRUIT CUP

LUNCH: SALAD WITH SLICED CHICKEN BREAST

SNACK: PEANUTS AND GRAPES

DINNER: LEAN STEAK/ YAM/ VEGGIES

DAY 10:   BREAKFAST: TURKEY BACON AND EGG WHITES 2

SNACK: YOGURT WITH FRUIT

LUNCH: CHICKEN BREAST WITH VEGGIES

SNACK: JELLO

DINNER: GRILLED FISH AND VEGGIES

DAY 11:   BREAKFAST: 2 CUPS OF COLD CEREAL WITH BERRIES

SNACK: STRAWBERRY SHAKE

LUNCH: YOGURT/ FRUIT/ VEGGIE WITH 1 CUP OF BROWN RICE

SNACK: CHICKEN SANDWICH

DINNER: BEANS AND RICE/ VEGGIES

DAY 12:   BREAKFAST: BOILED EGG WITH BANANA

SNACK: SMOOTHIE

LUNCH: SALAD

SNACK: MIXED FRUIT

DINNER: CHICKEN BREAST SANDWICH WITH 1 CUP OF VEGGIES

DAY 13:   BREAKFAST: CEREAL

SNACK: CELERY STICK WITH YOGURT

LUNCH: 1 SMALL VEGGIE BURGER WITH BROWN RICE

SNACK: CHEESE STICKS WITH VEGGIES

DINNER: MEATBALLS WITH BROWN RICE

DAY 14:   BREAKFAST: BANANA AND STRAWBERRIES

SNACK: PROTEIN SHAKE

LUNCH: TURKEY SANDWHICH WITH VEGGIES

SNACK: PEAR OR FRESH FRUIT OPTIONAL

DINNER: CHICKEN STIR FRY WITH VEGGIES

DAY 15:   BREAKFAST: PORFAIT YOGURT

SNACK: SHAKE

LUNCH: BROWN RICE/ VEGGIES

SNACK: LOWFAT PUDDING

DINNER: BAKED FISH/ BROWN RICE/ VEGGIES

DAY16:   BREAKFAST: YOGURT

SNACK: TRAIL MIX

LUNCH: SALAD

SNACK: MIXED FRUIT

DINNER: LASAGNA

DAY 17:   BREAKFAST: OATMEAL

SNACK: PEANUTS MIXED WITH RAISINS

LUNCH: TURKEY SANDWICH/ FRUIT/ WATER MELON SLICES

SNACK: SMOOTHIE

DINNER: GRILLED SALMON/ ASPARAGUS SPEAR/ APPLESAUCE

DAY 18:   BREAKFAST: BANANA AND STRAWBERRIES

SNACK: GRANOLA/ BERRIES/ VEGGIES

LUNCH: TACOS

SNACK: CHEESE STICKS WITH VEGGIES

DINNER: SALMON CAKES/ BROWN RICE/ VEGGIES

DAY 19:   BREAKFAST: CEREAL WITH BERRIES

SNACK: SHAKE

LUNCH: SALAD

SNACK: FRUIT

DINNER: PORK LION/ BROCCOLI/ APPLESAUCE

DAY 20:   BREAKFAST: BOILED EGG WITH BANANA

SNACK: PROTEIN BAR

LUNCH: VEGGIE SOUP

SNACK: SMOOTHIE

DINNER: BAKED CHICKEN QUARTER/ CAULIFLOWER/ YAM POTATO

DAY 21:   BREAKFAST: OMELET

SNACK: SMOOTHIE

LUNCH: SALAD

SNACK: FRUIT

DINNER: FISH/ 2 CUPS OF VEGGIES

DAY 22:   BREAKFAST: CEREAL

SNACK: CELERY WITH PEANUT BUTTER

LUNCH: GRILLED CHEESE SANDWHICH ITH SOUP

SNACK: SHAKE

DINNER: GRILLED CHICKEN WITH VEGGIES

DAY 23:   BREAKFAST: YOGURT AND BANANA

SNACK: PEANUTS AND FRUIT

LUNCH: HAM SANDWHICH/ 1 PIECE OF FRUIT/ SOUP

SNACK: PEPPERONI WITH DICED CHEESE CHEDDAR

DINNER: LEAN STEAK/ 2 CUPS OF VEGGIES

DAY 24:   BREAKFAST: OATMEAL

SNACK: YOGURT

LUNCH: PROTEIN SHAKE

SNACK: FRUIT

DINNER: VEGGIE BURGER/ BROWN RICE/ VEGGIES

DAY 25:   BREAKFAST: WHOLE WHEAT PANCAKES/ TURKEY BACON

SNACK: GRONOLA BAR WITH OGURT

LUNCH: TURKEY SANDWHICH WITH FRUIT CUP

SNACK: GRONOLA BAR WITH YOUGURT

DINNER: SALAD WITH SLICE CHICKEN BREAST/ LOW FAT DRESSING/ VEGGIES

DAY 26:   BREAKFAST: BOILED EGGS / FRUIT

SNACK: GRONOLA BAR

LUNCH: ROASRT BEEF SANDWHICH/ VEGGIES

SNACK: SMOOTHIE

DINNER: GRILLED FISH/ VEGGIES

DAY 27:   BREAKFAST: OATMEAL

SNACK: SHAKE

LUNCH: PEANUT BUTTER AND JELLY

SNACK: RICE CAKE AND ALMOND BUTTER

DINNER: WHOLE WHEAT PASTA WITH TOMATO SAUCE/ DICED CHICKEN

DAY 28:   BREAKFAST: YOGURT

SNACK: HALF APPLE AND CHEESE MOZZARELLA STICK

LUNCH: CHICKEN SANDWICH/ FRUIT CUP

SNACK: APPLES AND PEANUT BUTTER

DINNER: TUNA CASSEROLE

DAY 29:   BREAKFAST: CEREAL

SNACK: PEANUTS/ FRUIT

LUNCH: SALAD

SNACK: SMOOTHIE

DINNER: CHICKEN PARMESAN WITH WHOLE WHEAT PASTA

DAY 30:   BREAKFAST: FRENCH TOAST WITH STRAWBERRIES

SNACK: FRUIT

LUNCH: TURKEY SANDWICH/ FRUIT CUP

SNACK: CELERY/ PEANUT BUTTER

DINNER: TACOS WITH VEGGIES

BE SURE TO DRINK UP TO 8 OZ'S OF WATER PER DAY, AVOID FOODS HIGH IN FAT. MONITOR SALT INTAKE AND CHOOSE MEATS LOW IN FAT. AVOID FOOD AND DRINKS SUCH AS COFFEE AND SODAS, TOO MUCH FAST FOODS AND RED MEATS. WATCH YOUR WEIGHT AND CHECK YOUR BLOOD PRESSURE REGULARLY.

INTIMIDATION

Intimidation is something that you see on a daily basis and around the world. Sometimes you see it on television from boxing matches where one guy is trying... everywhere else in this country. According to Webster's dictionary, to intimidate is to make timid or fearful, frighten, to compel, or deter by or as if by threats and aggressive behavior. Sometimes the person who is trying to intimidate may not be a fighter at all but may have friends to help them out while you are by yourself. He or she may have a knife or a gun which in no way guarantees you a fair fight. In other instances, some people just know how to play crazy. There is a saying by James... so long because just like bullies you will eventually meet your match. The best way to combat intimidation is to not give into fear. It is okay to be fearful because that is your bodies natural reaction and warning signs telling you that something bad is about to happen. However, do not give into the fear that someone else is trying to inflict or instill in you. Believe it or not as fearful as you may appear the other person is just as afraid. This is why there is a period of arguing and build up before any punches

30 DAY STRENGTH/ CONDITIONING ROUTINE

DAY 1:   KICKBOXING

DAY 2:   STRECHING

DAY 3:   STRENGTH TRAIN- ARMS/ SHOULDERS

DAY 4:   SIT UPS/ PUSH UPS/ DOWNWARD DOGS YOGA

DAY 5:   LUNGES/ CALF RAISES/ SQUATS

DAY 6:   REST

DAY 7:   STRETCH

DAY 8:   CARDIO WORKOUT- TIRE HOPS

DAY 9:   STRETCH

DAY 10:   STRENGTH TRAIN/ BACK/ MOUNTAIN CLIMBER

DAY 11:   HOPS/ KICKS/ BEAR CRAWLS/ SNAKE WALKS

DAY 12:   WORK OUT WITH BROOM STICK/ JUMPING JAXS

DAY 13:   PUSH UPS/ SIT UPS/ BURPIES

DAY 14:   LEG LIFTS/ KNEE RAISES/ HIP ESCAPES

DAY 15:   REST

DAY 16:   STRETCH

DAY 17:   JOGGING/ TWISTS/ SQUATS

DAY 18:   SHADOW BOXING/ KNEE STIKES PRACTICE

DAY 19:   STRENGHT TRAINING/ ARM CURLS/ WRIST CURLS/ TRICEPS

DAY 20:   FRONT ROLL/ BACK ROLL/ SHOULDER ROLL

DAY 21:   KICKBOXING

DAY 22:   REST

DAY 23:   STRETCH

DAY 24:   CARDIO WORKOUT/ LUNGES

DAY 25:   SIT UP/ PUSH UPS/ SQUATS

DAY 26:   SHADOWBOXING/ PUNCHING BAG

DAY 27:   FRONT KICKS/ BACK KICKS/ SIDE KICKS

DAY 28:   STRENGTH TRAIN ARMS/ SQUATS/ FULL BODY OPTIONAL

DAY29:   REST

DAY 30:   STRETCH

FIGHT OR FLIGHT

In many ways, the idea of the fight or flight scenario consist of you being brave and standing up to engage another individual in combat or you simply run and find a safe location to prevent your opponent from hurting you while you call for help or the police. I would suppose the question are concern would be to determine which one is the best-case scenario. In many ways, it all depends on the situation, meaning that if you are outnumbered or overmatched and the person is carrying a weapon these reasons may give you the need to take flight and seek help. The fight aspect is best when both parties are evenly matched and no one else is seeking to jump into the physical exchange making it a fair fight. Keep in mind a fight does not always have to be physical. Sometimes a fight maybe a verbal or heated argument between two parties in which no physical blows occur. Most police officers like to use the fight or flight scenario because there are times for you to stand up and do battle but there are times in which you have to be smart and not be a superhero that involves him or her retreating and radioing for backup to resolve an issue that could turn into a fight or arrest. Although fighting in public is not legal, unfortunately it still happens all to often in schools, night clubs, on the street and in public places. As a result, there are usually groups of people watching, not trying to stop the fight and posting the fight on social media outlets for more likes. The sad thing is it is not until someone gets seriously injured or a death occurs that people end up regretting their role of encouraging the fight and doing nothing to prevent it in the first place.

Next, the police are called or paramedics come to assists the injured party and no one opens their mouth about what happened due to possible fear of retaliation are the same thing happening to them or their love ones.

I will always say that the stop snitching stance that young people use is the most stupid and ridiculous way to handle incidents where someone that they may know gets seriously harmed, injured or killed and not tell for fear of being called a rat or worse. This is a civilized society and people and communities need to stand up against this as a whole and hold individuals accountable for their actions. Moreover, fighting is not a part of normal human behavior, for the most part it is learned. There is nothing wrong with fighting for what you believe, but it should be done in a way that is peaceful and does not get innocent people hurt. In today's society people want to fight and debate about everything, even though debating is fine once the situation starts to escalate and turn into a confrontation it is best practice to either change the subject and focus on more productive matters at hand. However, you cannot stop all fights and fights are going to occur in your presence. Just because someone wants to fight you this does not mean you have to entertain their aggression. It is far wiser to be the bigger person and walk away cautiously. Once you have walked away and the individual becomes persistent in which he or she continues to engage you by blocking your path and challenging you, at this moment it would be appropriate to become the wolf. If you are an officer or military person you have to fight because not doing so may cause you to lose your life since the number one priority is making sure you come home safe. For everyday civilians' exposure to violence is always prevalent and the possibility of becoming a victim of some sort of violent situation can at times appear to be imminent or too easily possible. In many ways, just looking at the news can make an individual terrified and almost afraid to leave their home or go out late at night. As officers, our job is to protect the streets so that civilians no matter color, race or creed feels protected and not exposed to so much violence. Now how does this interpret to martial arts? The answer is train to learn how to fight and protect yourself against a would-be attacker. But if you are able to resolve the issue verbally by showing discipline and not showing how tuff you are is a big thing. Only use your skills when there is no other way to walk away and communication is not possible. If the person seriously assaults you control the individual until the police arrive and provide them with a statement of what just occurred. If help is available use it, if you can create distance or evade the individual do so and call for help. Martial Arts is about creating a safe community and ensuring that people have the ability and tools to protect themselves in times of need and if he or she finds their self in danger don't be afraid to fight back when necessary.

MARTIAL ARTS VS. MMA

The world of martial arts is unique in which there are various forms and disciplines to practice. For example, there is Taekwondo, Hapkido, Karate, Kenpo, Judo and other forms of techniques. For the most part, each technique has its own strength and weaknesses. In some forms of discipline, the focus is mainly geared towards kicking, doing katas and making loud breathing sounds, whereas some of the others consist of throws, strikes, and sweeps. There has always been question as to which martial arts is the best and at different sport events and competitions these styles have been used to compete against each other. The biggest event to date has been on the big stage of the UFC. The UFC stands for the Ultimate Fighting Championships which was banned for years due to some of the bloody competitive matches seen by viewers around the world. Due to popular demand the UFC has made a significant comeback with sanctions by the athletics commission and newly improved rules and regulations in which most matches are seen worldwide around the globe through apps and various cable channels. During each match competitors would compete against each other until the person with the best technique and endurance won. The winner would win a trophy with a check. In the beginning the person to win the most was Royce Gracie who was a Brazilian Jiu Jitsu Black Belt practitioner. In many ways, he proved to the world that the techniques and skills of Brazilian Jiu Jitsu was far more superior than some of the other styles. In fact, the only other styles that came close were boxing, Muay Thai and wrestling competitors. After seeing many wins from

Royce Gracie and the Brazilian Jiu Jitsu camp many perceived Brazilian Jiu Jitsu to be the style to use in combat especially since a lot of the focus involved clinching and taking the person to the ground to complete the submission. Many of the other styles focused squarely on stand up besides Judo and Wrestling. Today, the sport has evolved and there continues to be wins gained from competitors who are well rounded. Well rounded simply means that the individual is not a one-dimensional fighter, he or she may have a Black Belt in some other form of martial art but is familiar or verse in different styles and techniques. For example, you may have a boxer who is decent at stopping takedowns and have some forms of wrestling capabilities. Also, you may have a Muay Thai person who may be able to submit you with some form of judo or Brazilian Jiu jitsu move. This is part of a hyper training method that continues to grow, the only downfall is that some may choose not to pursue black belts in other martial arts because they may feel it is pointless since they may already know some of the most effective techniques. Truth is that martial arts and mixed martial arts are always evolving and new moves and techniques are being added on a consistent basis. For the most part it is important to stay current so that you do not open yourself to an easy defeat. Even if you are defeated, it's an opportunity to learn so you never really lose. When it comes to martial arts and mixed martial arts, there is always something to learn and add to your own craft. The techniques that are gaining a lot of attention right now is Sambo which is a Russian style of martial arts consisting of multiple leg lock submissions that are very painful to one's ligaments if you are unable to escape or fail to tap. I for one prefer not to compete in competitions where leg submissions are allowed but there are times while sparring at the gym or competing at annual promotions that an attempt will be made by me are the other person. If it is a concern and you are not that good at leg locks then focus on escapes and check out some of the moves and escapes on YouTube to familiarize and not leave yourself open for a quick leg lock submission. For me I respect the field of martial arts and with that being said I consider myself a martial artist who practice in all areas of martial arts and seek to grow and develop throughout the years to come. That being said, no one martial art is the best, you should choose a primary discipline to get your black belt and seek to practice other techniques and styles. Don't be one dimensional, continue to grow, things are always changing and most importantly never stop training.

DEALING WITH BULLIES

Most bullies are cowards because they tend to pick on people who are not in a position to defend themselves or they pick on people who they can easily outnumber and beat on. Usually, bullies do not pick on people their own size nor people who may evenly match them. Bullying has become an American epidemic in this country in which more cases of bullying are coming into the forefront. In many ways, bullying has gone mainstream from cyber bullying, workforce bullying, school yard bullying, street bullying and bullying in various spaces where people are in fear of someone and especially social media. Back in the day parents would tell their kids that if someone tries to bully them hit first and ask questions later but, in this era, we as a society have become so politically correct. Meaning that instead of standing up to bullies we walk away, run and hide, commit suicide or try to shy away from the bully hoping that he or she will move to someone else and not you so that you can be left alone. The truth is that most bullies will not stop messing with you until you take a stand against them. Of course, no one is encouraging violence however there are situations where you will need to defend yourself against a bully or bullies to prevent serious harm. Every situation is different in which some cases you may only need to speak your mind and walk away. However, there are times where you may not be able to simply walk away because the bully is continuing to taunt you, harass you and make threats against you. Now there are times where friends, family or associates may be able to get involved to prevent any situation from occurring but don't depend on that only. Sometimes the group or people may be encouraging the physical altercation instead of trying to prevent any violence from happening. The best policy is to always be ready regardless and watch your back. There are all types of bullies out there, some are sneaky, opportunistic and most of all cowards. They will do whatever they have to in order to make you either fear them, avoid them, run from them or make your life miserable. Whatever you do, do not allow this to happen because once you do that it becomes psychological. Unfortunately, this leads to you being afraid to come outside, socialize or even suicidal. Being bullied can be a humiliating thing but don't worry because you are not the only one being bullied. If the bully is messing with you more than likely they have been bullied themselves and in order for them to not feel bullied they have to bully someone else as a way to get through life. Also, more than likely the bully is miserable and simply jealous of you and want you to feel the same way by not being able to enjoy your life. Maybe you come from a nice family, wear nice clothes or simply you're are a nice person. Bullies are only happy when they are intimidating people or bragging about how they were able to intimidate somebody else. Moreover, because most people are just like sheep, they will follow that bully's behavior because he or she does not want to be on that bullies' bad side or become a victim themselves. Of course, as the saying goes "better you than me" and this becomes the scenario for each situation. This has been the case for years and it is only going to get worst before it gets any better. In our schools' young children are committing suicide and not wanting to go to school due to bullying. One may think that once you become an adult bullying disappears however in today's society this is far from the case. Today, you can see bullying on Instagram, reality tv shows, aggressive driving incidents, night clubs, domestic violence situations and in many other ways. Bullying has become a culture phenomenon where it puts one side against the other. Good news is more and more people are becoming sick and tired of bullies and they are standing up and calling it out on social media, tv shows and going as far as to report situations to the proper authorities to press charges. Now of course once you report situations to the authorities you may be accused of being a snitch or afraid that by doing so it may make you less popular with the people you know but who cares. My parents use to always say "you came into this world by yourself and you will leave this world by yourself". Most of those so-called friends will not be around once you are out of school anyway or change your location. If you are being bullied surround yourself with good and positive people who really have your back. Even if it's just your parents, guidance counselor, teacher, or whomever you may trust. More importantly, stand your ground with that bully by not allowing him to punk you or try to make you afraid. If the situation becomes violent protect yourself the best way you know how and report the incident to prevent it from happening again. If it does happen again make sure that the person is arrested and fill out a Protection Order to ensure that the individual is not permitted to come close to you or contact with you in anyway or risk incarceration. This applies to kids in schools and anywhere else that bullies may try to find their prey. More importantly, learn martial arts defense in order to even the odds and match whatever the bully may be trying to do, however if a weapon is involved, be smart, back away and call the Police!

BUILDING SELF CONFIDENCE

Trying to build self confidence comes from within. In many ways, it is the belief that you can conquer any situation or task that you are dealing with. Self confidence allows you to challenge situations without worrying about dangers that may exists. For instance, if you do martial arts and some strangers tries to assault you, you are less worried about what he or she may do to you, instead you may feel that the person may need to be more concerned about what you will do to them. When you have self-confidence, you have less fear or concern and you are surer about what you can do and not what they cannot do. Self confidence not only applies to martial arts but in everything you do. Self confidence is necessary in the workplace, business, fitness or any other place where you may feel challenged. In the workplace you need to have self confidence as a survival mechanism because you will need to perform on your job and your boss may ask or trust you to handle certain tasks that may be difficult. Often times those tasks include a bit of multi-tasking and at times can be more than one can handle. However, with self-confidence despite the excess workload you believe in yourself that you will complete your tasks and ensure that you do a good job. In business self confidence is important because you never know where your business is going to come from. You have to be able to sale yourself and convince people who are in business to do business with your company. If they feel that you did not sale your business strategies well on pitch, those clients will leave from the table and you will lose at closing that deal. Failure can at times lead to depression and a lack of self-confidence. The best thing you can do is "get back on that horse" meaning Get Up, dust yourself off and get back to it. If you wait too long you will give up on yourself and throw all of your talent away. In fitness, self confidence will be necessary especially if you are trying to lose weight to either model for pictures, magazines or some other health and fitness reason. One thing you can not do is listen to the nay Sayers. There will always be people out there who will still call you fat, you of shape or that they really cannot see the results that you desire. Do your best to ignore those idiots and focus on your goal. Don't be deterred by someone else's ignorance. Truth is you don't need to have all the physical definition in the world to be fit for the matter. Be the best healthy you, you can be and when you do reach your goal don't be afraid to show your results and share testimonials about your journey because in many situations some may have had to change their entire lifestyle to health due to illness, diabetes or other genetic circumstances. We all come in different shapes and sizes and you can never please everyone. As long as you maintain yourself confidence you are bound to be successful at achieving your goal. This is also true in martial arts. Self confidence in martial arts is important because you are learning how to defend yourself against a would-be attacker. Most of the time you may only need to use your skills in the gym but there are situations where you may become bullied by someone at a gas station, convenience store, 7 eleven, traffic situation or etc. Of course, you will do your best to avoid any violence however there are situations where the use of your skills may become apparent and necessary to save your life. This applies to those in law enforcement as well. You never know who is going to try to test you in a physical altercation. Possibly, an inmate, a person you are taking into custody or someone who just does not like cops or anyone in uniform who work for the government. Every situation is different but your ability to handle each incident and have the self-confidence to control certain matters is a true sign of growth and abilities.

BRUCE LEE'S CONCEPTS AND PHILOSOPHIES

" Boards don't hit back" is one of my favorite Bruce Lee phrases from the movie "Enter the Dragon". This phrase was unique at a time when some martial arts forms were not being tested and tried. At tournaments, everything would be no contact but you would earn points for attempted strikes. Most of the matches were won that way and the school with the most winners would get the recognition and trophy. In many ways, Bruce Lee was the 1st to implement full contact martial arts as demonstrated in some of his earlier videos. My impression of what he meant in regards to boards don't hit back is that one must try to make contact to prove that he or she will defeat the other person. The other competitor may move out the way and counter with a strike or the person may miss and try some other finishing technique. Bruce Lee shutdown the nay Sayers who felt that you must be a black belt to teach martial arts. Bruce Lee incorporated boxing, fencing, Gung Fu and other strengths and weaknesses from other martial arts to create his own Jeet Kune Do style. An even greater asset was his ability to teach and demonstrate his art form against any and all challengers to prove that what he was saying was indeed effective. Another concept from Bruce Lee is to be like water You must adapt to the various changes in martial arts, don't be one dimensional, if it works use it and not use things that do not work. One of Bruce Lee's greatest revelations was his health and fitness regimen.

He would practice his techniques with regularity, exercise and monitor his overall diet and intake.

Back then many of the martial arts instructor's focus were not on health and nutrition. Many of them were skillful and overweight. In many of Bruce Lee's movies he would demonstrate his speed and agility in his kicks, punches and strikes. In addition, he would show his level of fitness from his physique and endurance. One of the concepts I admired most is his mindset and attitude towards combat and competing. One of Bruce Lee's quotes is "Defeat is a state of mind, no one is ever defeated until defeat has been accepted as a reality. According to this statement, if you are defeated it is an opportunity to learn from your mistake. If you allow yourself to think you are defeated you will lose and miss out on the opportunity to learn. Defeat is a state of mind but you must maintain the mindset of winning. If you lose that is a great time for you to practice your art and be even more determined to defeat your opponent. Bruce Lee's philosophies and concepts are very important because even in today's martial arts there is still argument over when it is okay to teach or open up your own school. This is creating issues for those with lower belts who may be competent in martial arts and already have a school or academy to compete with those who are already black belts. This black belt situation was mostly the case for Japanese style of martial arts but not so much for others. I believe that when you feel that you are ready to open up a school you should but it does not help that some martial art federations are putting bans on lower belts teaching, this makes it difficult to run a legitimate school if you are not a black belt. In so many ways, this goes against Bruce Lee tradition and puts things back into a situation where anyone calling themselves a black belt can dominate the martial arts world while you sit on the sidelines to open up a school or business. The situation such as this has not become widespread yet but it is definitely going global in this day and age of social media. I feel that there is opportunity for everyone and if you enjoy teaching martial arts, no one should interfere with it and allow you to compete and flourish in the markets besides monopolies are banned as well and competition is good for business all around because t gives people choices and the freedom to learn from whomever he or she wants.

STREET FIGHTING VS. SPORTS JIU JITSU, ARE THEY THE SAME THING?

The answer is no, a street fighter is not worried about using techniques or special skills they Are just trying to win the fight so he or she may use anything and everything to win. In sports Jiu jitsu there are rules, no groin strikes, eye gouging and you get points. Also, in sport Jiu jitsu you can finish a guy but do not pull guard in a street fight, otherwise you risk getting body slammed on your head. In a street fight you are fighting more for survival and to defeat your opponent, in sports Jiu jitsu you are not as focused on survival instead you just want to win the match or defend well and get a medal, belt or trophy.

There is no concern of life or death type situations for sports Jiu jitsu however you can be injured if you refuse to tap. Another difference is that a street fighter has no belt rank and plain clothes is usually the preference. In sports Jiu jitsu there is focus on your belt rank and sometimes there may be special rules in regards to the Gi you are wearing which may in some cases cause you to lose your match if you are in violation. When a street fight occurs, there is no preparation and it usually happens when you least expect, not feeling well, not in the mood or just plain anoid or agitated about something else. Usually, when your doing sports Jiu jitsu you have time to prepare and strategize what you may want to do in your match. The part that is interesting is that once you get into a physical exchange most of what you practiced will go out the window but hopefully if your skilled enough your opponent will create an opening or you will go back to your technique and finish him or him off. For a street fighter finishing you off may be a knockout, body slam, choking you unconscious or simply punking you, bullying you or trying to intimidate the individual. For sports Jiu jitsu the focus is on maintaining discipline and defending yourself against people who try to bring you harm by using real life effective techniques to defeat your opponent without doing all of the extra stuff in a street fight. Street fights can be dangerous but the only way to prepare for them is to make sure that you are training in some type of art form. One thing not to overlook is size and weight because this does matter. If the guy is taller or bigger then you may want to focus on defending than taking advantage of openings to finish him or her off. If you are bigger and the opponent is smaller, be the elephant not the ant. Use your size and weight to defeat or control your opponent. More importantly, don't be a bully, if your winning the fight then try to settle things down so that your opponent may feel some honor in defeat instead of being disgraced. Most disgraced people will always hold on to the grudge and try to attack you when you least expect. One of my favorite scene's in Way of the Dragon is when Bruce Lee had killed his opponent played by Chuck Norris and even though he won he still honored him by putting Chuck Norris Gi over his body, wrapping his belt neatly and bowing to him as a show of respect. Now I'm not saying you need to do all of that but allow the defeated person to be able to show face so that things do not come to a head again. Now if you have a person who continues to harass you despite having previous physical exchange a stay away order from the courts may be necessary to change the situation. Furthermore, street fighting is something you can not prepare for whereas in sports Jiu jitsu you can and include skills for you to finish your opponent, but keep in mind if you're not careful and not expecting a street fighter can get lucky by sucker punch and end up knocking you out.

BEING A MAT CHAMPION VS. TEACHING MIXED MARTIAL ARTS AND COMPETING!

A mat champion is someone who goes to the gym to train regularly but does not compete. He or she is in the gym day in and day out looking for people they can crush and get easy finishes because the others may not come to the gym as frequent. Most of the time mat champions will put expectations on you to compete but they will not do it themselves for fear of getting defeated in public. When you are teaching Mixed Martial Arts, you get to have a deeper understanding of techniques being seen and practiced. It is very important to not wait until you are a Black Belt to teach because if you are not use to talking in front of groups of people this can be problematic. Nothing is worse than having your instructor ask you to teach a class and not knowing the first place to start. Especially to the lower belts because even though you have a Black Belt many of them will laugh at the fact that you do not seem confident in your teaching abilities. Truthfully, you should be teaching as you start progressing within your belt ranks. If your goal is to never teach and simply be a mat champion then you should consider competing so that you can help build the school and create worldwide recognition for the place you train at. There are plenty of instructors who will welcome a student who wins matches and get medals in competitions, it looks for magazines and it helps the school grow and receive good media attention. However, you must keep in mind that as you move up in rank the instructor will ask you and expect you to help with demonstrations. A good way to start would be with teaching one on one training sessions so that you can get through the stage freight and get use to teaching the curriculum. Now there are some people who have trouble speaking in front of others or large groups. In those cases, there is very little you can do because there may be a medical attachment issue where the person may sweat often, stamper or just say one thing and demonstrate another. Whatever the case may be, try to overcome this fear if you look forward to eventually teaching or opening up your own school. For years, the US was dominated by other forms of Martial Arts and many of them have come and gone. Now, Mixed Martial Arts is proving to be the people's choice to train in due to proven real-life techniques and self-defense. I say this because as the field continues to grow, there will be more and more instructors teaching and if this is something you want to do, don't wait till the last minute. Equally important is that if you seek to get a Black Belt and teach in Brazilian Jiu Jitsu you will need to wait 10 to 12 years before you reach Professor level two stripes and open up a reputable school. If you are able to put the time on the mat to reach this point then such would be a huge accomplishment. Most of all train and enjoy yourself but be open minded to the possibilities because they are truly endless.

PREPARING YOUR MIND FOR BATTLE

In many ways, preparing yourself for battle can be difficult because most physical exchanges are spontaneous, you may not have time to ready yourself. In addition, the situation alone may make you nervous or have some kind of anxiety. The most important thing you can do is not go into the situation worried about whatever the other person can do to you. Your focus should be on winning, protecting yourself and surviving that physical exchange. If the person is getting the best of you, you will have to adapt or change what you are doing so that the other person has less of an advantage.

For example, in one of my Purple Belt Competitions I had a guy taking me down multiple times with the same exact takedown technique but whenever I tried to take him down, I had difficulty. The match was going so fast and we were running out of time. Over and over I found myself on my back defending. At the end of the fight I lost but once I got a chance to rethink the match, I figured that once he took me down the first and second time, I should have used some takedown defense so that every time he would shoot towards my legs, he would eventual tire himself out. This would have given me more time to figure out a way to reverse the situation and get top control on my opponent or at least side control, then go for the finish.

Anytime you go into battle you never know what to expect but you can adapt to the circumstances as long as no weapons are involved, multiple attackers or elements of surprise. Some people thank that if you appear afraid or fearful of your opponent then that is a sign of weakness. I believe in Rickson Gracie's philosophy in that fear is your bodies way of warning you that something is going to happen. The more that you are able to overcome your fear in battle the greater chance of success against your opponent. Unless he or she is too over-skilled and you are so exhausted that you have completely gassed yourself out.

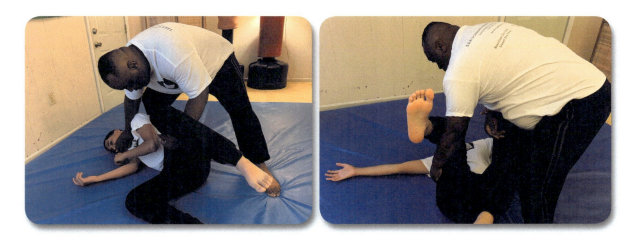

This happens a lot in tournament challenges. You will be completely gassed out from fighting one opponent after the other but the good thing is the more you do the less nervous you are so preparing your mindset is not such a difficult task because of your familiarity. For others who may be new to competing in tournaments or maybe never been involved in a street fight, simply not freezing up and doing something can be the challenge. Whatever the case is if you think that you are going to lose you probably will.

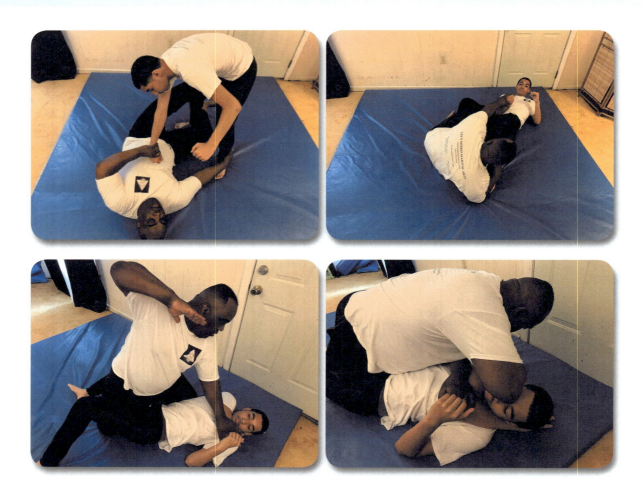

In my line of work as a Public Safety Officer, I get radio calls all the time to deal with urgent situations, sometimes physical and others not so much. I do realize that mindset is everything and when you are battling on the front lines as a first responder you have to do whatever is necessary to come home, so a winning mindset is key and a dose of courage is never a bad thing when you are in a battle. More importantly, learn skills and train but don't forget to fight back!

ADAPTING TO THE ENVIROMENT, DON'T GO TO THE GROUND FOR FREE!

Most people are afraid to go to the ground in a fight for fear of being stomped or kicked in the face or other areas of the body, I have seen people just cover up or put their knees and elbows together to prevent from taking excessive blows. Then in some cases, there are some who will simply get up and run away, the ground game can be tricky in that if you are not aware of what you are doing the other person can get an advantage on you with just a little bit of wrestling skills or simply be bigger and stronger than you are. The best thing you can do is learn how to protect yourself on the ground even if this is the only way to develop ground defense skills, something is better than nothing. Now, I'm not talking about watching tv and trying to use them in real life, you need to get some kind of training so that you can skillfully defend yourself on the ground. Especially since most street fights end up on the ground anyway. Ground defense is good because this will help you avoid being taken to the ground and allow you to keep standing up which may or may not increase your chances of winning the match. For me, I never underestimate anyone's ability, I just focus on winning. Moreover, if you get traditional ground training you will know how to protect yourself on the ground and the best way to finish your opponent is by choking them unconscious, submission or control holds. In other words, you will have more options when it comes to finishing the fight. In addition, ground training will help you to adopt to your environment during the physical exchange. In most fights, you will start by standing, one person hits the other, some wrestling may ensue then go immediately to ground, against the wall or into a bunch of onlookers yelling and screaming during the fight. Bottom line, no one wants to look like they just got their ass whipped in front of a crowd of people. Also, you will look good in front of onlookers for standing up for yourself and showing a decent level of skill. Beware of objects if the fight goes to the ground because their may be broken glass from pictures, bottles chairs or just simply a mess from all the constant movement. In a street fight there is a lot of movement, you are never in the same place the fight started in. More importantly, if there are other attackers be aware of this, try to get to your feet, do the most damage to the one close to you so that the others may decide to back off. Get yourself someplace safe and call the Police or simply get away as quickly as you can because it is no longer a fair fight anyway. Ground training is definitely becoming a big thing so that people are not so one dimensional, but the one to be clear on is that a sucker punch does not require skill so watch your distance and keep your hands up, if it goes to the ground be prepared and be ready to move around the room. If you can finish the person by submission, do so if not control that individual until he or she gives up or quit.

ALWAYS PROTECT YOURSELF AND DEFEND YOURSELF

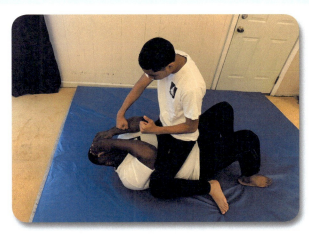

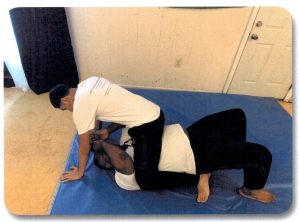

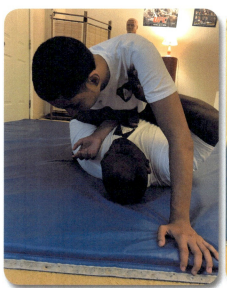  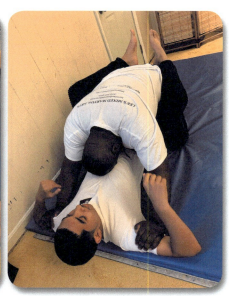

These days people are very unpredictable, someone you think you have a good relationship with will turn on you and next thing you know your getting a bottle struck across your head or a fist to your face or simply a standoff to see who is going to strike first. You see this time and time again on reality tv shows and in real life. On reality tv shows this is always the case to get more ratings and draw in more controversy but in real life the situation can be a little tricky. For instance, due to maturity and trying to be the bigger person there may be some delay in reaction time. Especially, if one has more to lose than the other. The last thing you want to do is go from being a responsible adult to sitting in a jail cell because you got into a dispute with some random idiot in a club or on the street. The main thing to ask yourself is if the situation is worth it, if you are in immediate danger or if you can simply walk away from the situation. If the answer is no to all of these questions then you may have no choice but to defend yourself. Now some may feel that asking yourself all these questions before you have a fight with someone is weak and does not look as tough. I say you should never go into any situation not thinking because if someone calls the Police and the both of you are arrested, you want to be on the winning side where your defense is that you were trying to defend yourself while the other person continued to be the aggressor. You may want to even specify different things that you tried to say or do to avoid confrontation in the first place. This way you get to win twice. The law allows you to protect yourself if you believe that you were in immediate danger or felt fear for your life or personal safety. This is good because if you're not careful you risk the other individual claiming a mutual combat situation and risks both of you being charged with a Felony Disorderly Conduct charge that will stay on your record for a long period of time. I've seen cases where this has happened in court where the person was trying to defend themselves but due to a lack of evidence, both people were charged. The end result was a court fine, no contact but with the charge still being on their record even with being placed on probation or pre-trial services. I will always tell people to protect yourself and defend yourself because this can be a means of survival.

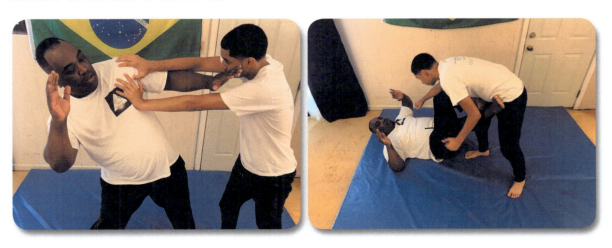

For instance, if the person keeps getting close to you or putting their hand in your face when you told them to stop or back up. The alarm in your head should be to protect and defend yourself. If you can, avoid hitting the other person first but if you fear getting sucker punched because the other person is up close and trying to intimidate you by grabbing and pulling at you then you may have no other choice. Now if you're at work and you are working somewhere where you can get hired help because it's not worth you losing your job or being on the news due to some type of excessive force situation use it. In an effort to defend and protect yourself, it is always good to maintain your fitness and enroll in some kind of self-defense classes or ground and boxing training.

More importantly, if you can avoid the fight all together this may be the best option but you should never get too comfortable as a grown up to think that no one will challenge you because of your age. I had a guy in his 20's challenge me in my 40's. It surprised me at first but not so much because at this time I was working in a jail. I chose to use the hired help but some of my co workers where critical because some felt that I should have done more by taking the guys head off for daring to challenge me in the first place and being a big bad ass martial artist. In general, I'm a family man, and I never condone violence unless it is absolutely necessary and I believe life is about choices. In that situation I felt that a physical exchange was not necessary because I was not in any immediate danger and hired help was available.

Getting into a full physical exchange may have been messy, showing off and putting my job at risk. Now if the young challenger would have tried to swing on me, I would have had no other choice but to inflict serious pain on him. It was just with knowing that in this instance I was able to be the bigger person, lead by example in which the young man later apologized and we were able to move on in a positive way. Even more interesting, that was the shortest report that I ever wrote with little to no contact. Every situation is different, for me if you can write you can fight, especially in my profession.

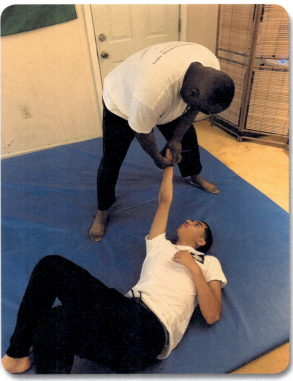

However, if you are a civilian, don't go into a situation blind, ask yourself those questions, is the person worth it, am I in immediate danger or can I walk away. If the answer is no, do what you have to do to survive that situation and have someone call the Police before things get too dangerous. Most people will cheer on a fight but very few will try to help even if the other person is not fighting fair, maybe with a knife, other attackers or worse a gun. Always be careful protect yourself and defend yourself when necessary, be humble but no body's Punk!

SELF DEFENSE

It is always a good idea to practice self- defense. Self- defense teaches you awareness and it allows you to defend yourself while attempting to escape. When doing self-defense against someone you're not looking to get into a full out brawl or fight you are just trying to protect yourself from serious injury or harm. However, there are some instances where you may need to use self defense against a violent encounter. In many rape cases victims have had to use self defense techniques against a violent assailant. In addition, in many domestic violence cases self defense moves were used to fend off their attacker however in some cases weapons such as a knife or gun were presented in which the victim may have either lost their life or became seriously injured. The one thing I will say though is that knowing something is better than not knowing anything. We live in a dangerous society in which everything is violent, in schools, churches, television, video games, movies and in other places. You never know if once you step out of your own door or come back from a long trip if someone is lurking in your backdoor or you might get into a fight with someone at a gas station or at a grocery store while standing in line for a long period of time. Over the years I have noticed people's patience have just diminished into bad behavior and everything must be resolved with violence. You would think that as two adults one should be able to work things out before it leads to violence but this is not the case in many instances. Just because the they are in an adult body or old as you this does not mean that he or she is mature and beneath getting into petty physical altercations with you. Some of the bigger situations that usually always turn aggressive is aggressive driving and causing an accident. While on duty, I reported to a call where a couple was arguing with this guy in his own car, somehow someone got out of their truck and before you know it gun shots were fired into the window. Luckily no one got killed but this situation is an example of how violent we have become as a society. Learning self-defense is beneficial because it's not a situation where you need to worry about getting a belt, you just show up in relax clothes or regular clothes and you practice the techniques demonstrated. The more you do the moves the greater your proficiency becomes. As a matter of fact, most Brazilian Jiu Jitsu gyms are requiring that you have a solid self defense game before you get your Black Belt. For me, I think you should do both if you have the time. Practice ground defense and training, then mix it up with a little self defense and boxing. The ground training will help you if someone tries to take you to the ground and hold you there. The boxing techniques is just good from striking awareness and to not get sucker punched. Self- defense is excellent to control the situation while standing up and allowing you to get away. The Gracie's have added a self defense and instructor program that demonstrates a lot of techniques that are useful for females to defend themselves. However, self defense is not just good for females, it's good for guys as well. There are techniques in self defense such as knee strikes, elbow strikes, punches and others that will keep guys interested and understanding the need to add it to their arsenal, especially trained Martial Artists. If you are not training in self defense you should be, it can only help you save your own life or someone else's.

EYE OF THE TIGER, MAINTAINING THAT WARRIOR SPIRIT

In many ways, eye of the tiger is a synonym for staying ready for battle. Eye of the tiger is showing no fear and displaying that outer toughness and stare that even the craziest person would be afraid to even try you. Sometimes in a stand off or matchup the stare down is the most telling. At times it's a great way to know or get a feeling for if our opponent is scared or unsure of themselves. Time and time again, I've watched boxing shows in which the sports correspondents can look at the person as they are walking down the aisle to enter the ring and they can tell whether the fighter is hungry or has a look like they really should not be there or may lose the fight. Usually they are correct because they analyze the fights quite often. I remember when buster Douglas fought Mike Tyson. In many ways, Buster Douglas had a very determined look on his face and he seemed like he was not afraid of anything, no one knew that he had lost a family member until after the fight. On the other hand, Iron Mike Tyson looked pretty sure of himself but nowhere as determined as buster Douglas that night. Through buster Douglass tenacity, determination and warrior spirit he was able to defeat Mike Tyson with a combination from out of this world causing one of the biggest upsets in the boxing worlds history. Mike Tyson was knocked out and he seemed to be wobbly at the end of the fight with a big not around his eye. The legal gamblers lost big that night because no one believed that Buster Douglas would pull off such an upset. This was a classic underdog type situation in which the least established fighter had little support with all the odds stacked against him while the more established fighter had all the support in the world and lost to the underdog in grand fashion. Absolutely, no one could believe that Mike Tyson had lost and the amount of news articles it would generate as a result around the world. One of my favorite eyes of the tiger moments is in the movie Rocky III when Rocky was beaten senseless by challenger Clubber Lane played by Mr. T himself and he was so afraid to lose what he had worked so hard to get in his boxing career that he was scared to fight him again. Later on, Apollo Creed would help Rocky train and get his confidence back by taking him to the trenches and away from all the flash and focus on winning. Even when Rocky and Clubber Lane squared off again Clubber Lane noticed an immediate change in Rocky's overall demeanor in which Rocky showed no fear and a determination in his eyes to not be timid or intimidated and to win the fight. For me, I embrace the warrior spirit in my competitions and while sparring in the gym against opponents. The way of the Bushido is the way of the warrior. You must fight back as if you are fighting for your life or as though you don't expect to live after your dual. In my profession I wear a side arm in which I try to be proficient with it the same way the Samurai's were proficient with there sword. In addition, I wear outside armor for protection along with weapons that can be used to combat an attack. The Samurai wore outside armor as well and they would have other hidden devices that were useful to combat attackers. I say this because the work of a public service officer is similar to that of a Samurai. You try to keep the peace but when danger arise you defend to the best of your ability even if that means sacrificing your life. I always say that if I'm going to go out, I want to be in full uniform, in a fierce battle, protecting the victim with dignity, respect and honor. Furthermore, I feel that this is the best way to honor the Way of the Samurai, Yasuke aka Black Samurai, keep the Eye of the Tiger and maintain the Warrior spirit within.

IN CONCLUSION

In conclusion, the purpose of this book is to provide a resource and survival guide for dealing with real everyday type situations that may or may not become violent. We live in a very violent society therefore it is necessary to be prepared by understanding your fears and knowing what to do about them when danger comes your way. In addition, there has always been this concern about a skilled martial artist verses a street fighter and whether or not the Martial Artists would automatically win because of his or her belt level. The answer is no, depending on the style of Martial Arts and skill level and other factors will determine the success against a street fighter. Know if the street fighter is not really skilled but is just a loud talker who likes to intimidate then by all means he or she will be easily defeated. Bruce Lee's philosophies are just as important today as they were back in the 1960's and 1970's. In many ways, he studied the art of fighting in great detail and he examined close combat techniques in a way like none other. Bruce Lee is without a doubt the Grandmaster of Mixed Martial Arts. The world of Mixed Martial Arts is continuing to grow and spreading throughout all cable networks. This is a long way away from where the sport was during its demise, for the most part the future is looking brighter and the possibility of the sport becoming a lifetime thing is a reality, similar to boxing. Bullying is a very sad reality in our society because nowadays little kids are becoming more fearful and suicidal due to bullying. This must and has to end sooner than later, no one should have to accept being bullied especially in a place where children are supposed to learn and be educated. Moreover, always remember to protect yourself and keep training because you never know when you could or might get involved an incident that you did not intend or expect. Self-defense is a great weapon to have in cases of unexpected attack however if the situation becomes deadly a more aggressive style of Martial Arts may be necessary. The great thing is that all Martial Arts have strengths and weaknesses so you can always try different ones to see which one is right for you are you can do like Bruce Lee and blend them into your own style. Whatever you do try to pick one style that you can become proficient in then add the others. Furthermore, Mindset, adapting to your environment and Eye of the Tiger are important elements to have when eliminating your opponent. Never worry about what he or she is going to do to you but he or she should be more worried about what you are going to do to them, be the Wolf not the Sheep!

Thanks to all of our Family, Friends and Supporters and everyone who believed in me making this Book and turning my dream into a reality!